HOW TO CLOTHBIND A PAPERBACK BOOK

A Step-by-Step Guide for Beginners

FRANCIS J. KAFKA

Dover Publications, Inc.

New York

To
Scott Michael Oslislo

Published in Canada by General Publishing Company, Ltd.,
30 Lesmill Road, Don Mills, Toronto, Ontario.
Published in the United Kingdom by Constable and Company, Ltd.

How to Clothbind a Paperback Book is a new work, first published by Dover Publications, Inc., in 1980.

International Standard Book Number: 0-486-23837-7
Library of Congress Catalog Card Number: 79-51883

Manufactured in the United States of America
Dover Publications, Inc.
180 Varick Street
New York, N.Y. 10014

Contents

	PAGE
Introduction	1
The Parts of a Book	3
Tools and Materials	5
Preparing the Contents for Binding	9
Drilling, Sewing, Rounding and Backing	11
Making the Case	13
Embellishing the Book	15
Casing the Book	17
Inserting the Endpapers	19
Making a Slipcase	21
Repairs	23
General Hints, Further Projects and Bibliography	25
Sources of Supply	25

Introduction

Bookbinding has its origins far back in antiquity, with the effort people made to gather up hand-lettered parchment leaves into a neat and orderly package which could be carried about. Medieval monks discovered how to stitch the leaves together and cover this "binding" with a parchment or leather case. The techniques which they used were handed down through the ages from master to apprentice, and remain virtually unchanged to this day.

The hobbyist who takes up this craft will find it enjoyable, relaxing and inexpensive. The basic skills required are relatively easy to master and can be practiced within a limited amount of space. Furthermore, the craft lends itself in a very accommodating way to the person who may not have endless hours to devote at one time. Many of the steps in bookbinding take less than an hour to accomplish, and then the work must be set aside for drying.

With the techniques described in this book, it is possible to clothbind a paperback book or rebind a clothbound volume. Instructions for several styles of binding are included, as well as information on how to make undetectable repairs on worn or damaged books.

Many of the tools required are household items: a hammer, hand drill, sewing needle, stout thread and sandpaper. Instructions are furnished (requiring few carpentry skills) on how to construct three additional items of equipment: a finishing press, box mortise and drilling jig. These, with a few further items to be purchased, constitute the tools of the craft. A chapter is devoted to tools and materials, and how to acquire them. The materials also tend to be inexpensive, and hints are included on how to salvage these to make for greater economy. Of course, the advanced hobbyist may want to spend considerably more money for fancy leather cover material and fine endpapers.

We hope you will find the instructions in this book clear and concise, and that through them you will gain a good knowledge of the rudiments of the craft. In the appendix to this volume is a list of books from which more advanced techniques can be learned. Also in the appendix is a list of suppliers who furnish materials and tools for bookbinding and repair. Read *all* the instructions contained herein before beginning work on a book.

1

The Parts of a Book

At the outset it will be helpful to define the different parts of a book and explain the various methods of modern book construction.

Figure 1 shows the outside of a clothbound book. It consists of two hinged *covers*, and the slightly convex section between the covers known as the *spine*. The top of the spine is called the *head* and the bottom is called the *tail*. The strip between the spine and covers is flexible and allows the covers to move: it is called the *hinge*. The entire covering, known as the *case*, is assembled in one piece before being attached to the pages of the book (the *contents*).

Figure 2 shows the inside of the same book, exposing the contents and the *endpapers*. Half of each endpaper is attached to the inside of the cover, while the other half is bound with the contents. It will be noticed in these illustrations that a decorative strip is attached to the head of the contents, next to the spine. This material is known as

headbanding and was originally used only at the head to give the book additional strength at the point where the book is grasped to be pulled from the shelf. Headbanding is now also used at the tail for the sake of symmetry. The contents of a book, when bound, have an exposed *top edge*, *bottom edge* and *fore edge*.

The book you buy in the bookstore today has been bound in one of three ways.

Most hardcover books and the best-quality paperbacks are *signature bound*. With this method groups of pages, called *signatures*, are successively sewn to each other until the entire contents have been assembled. The pages in each signature derive from a single large sheet of paper that has been fed through a printing press and then folded and refolded several times. It is then trimmed on three sides to give, typically, either 16, 32, or 64 consecutive pages. Signature groupings can usually be detected at the top or bottom

FIGURE 1

edge of the contents, next to the binding. If you are in doubt as to whether a book is signature bound, spread the contents of the book wide and search for the thread which binds the signatures together. Signature-bound books are the most durable: it is nearly impossible for a page to work itself loose from the binding.

Most of the mass market, small-sized paperbacks you find in drugstores, at newsstands and in bookstores are *perfect bound*. The designation "perfect" indicates not the quality of the binding, but the method by which signatures are trimmed on all four sides (cutting off the signature folds) and then glued directly into the spine. There is no internal network of connection provided by thread, and thus it is not uncommon for pages to detach themselves from the glue and fall out of the book. Perfect-binding techniques have improved dramatically in the last few years, and the techniques outlined here are as adequate to binding this type of book as for any other; but other considerations should make you think twice before binding a perfect-bound book. These books are often printed on inferior-quality paper, which will yellow and crumble prematurely in spite of the durable binding you apply. In addition, the margins in perfect-bound books are often too narrow to permit rebinding. If, when the book is opened flat, the inside margins appear adequate, you should then make a judgment as to the quality of the paper. Even if the paper is of poor quality you may want to rebind; the new binding will at least prolong the useful life of the book.

Magazines and magazine-sized books (with relatively few pages) are often *saddle-stitch bound* (or *saddle-wired*). Formerly done with thread, wire staples are most commonly used today. Signatures are trimmed and nested inside one another and then this spread stack of pages is placed on the V-shaped anvil of a wire-stitching machine. Staples are driven through the entire stack, including covers, and the pages are folded around the line of staples. Staples can be detected on the spine of such a book and between the two innermost pages. The book you are holding in your hands is saddle-stitched. Such books or magazines can be bound very successfully. Once again, let the size of the margins and the quality of the paper be your guide.

FIGURE 2

2
Tools & Materials

This chapter contains three sections which describe the tools, materials and equipment necessary to carry out the projects in this book. The first two sections (tools, materials) are annotated lists, with optional items ranked at the end of each list. The third section contains instructions on how to construct three pieces of equipment: the finishing press, box mortise and drilling jig. Purchased equipment may be substituted for these three pieces; however, the expense will be tremendous in comparison with the small amount of time and energy necessary for their construction.

BASIC BOOKBINDING TOOLS

Hammer. A ball-peen hammer is the best choice among household tools, but any hammer will suffice. A special bookbinder's hammer is illustrated in Figure 9, Chapter 3 of this book. It has a mushroom-shaped head which makes it ideal for the rounding and backing operation.

Sharp knife. A good penknife is the best choice because of its maneuverability. A paring knife or heavy matt knife is a good substitute. Some means of keeping the knife very sharp (whetstone, strop, etc.) is also necessary.

Scissors. They should be sharp and relatively large (dressmaker's shears, for example).

Plastic ruler. For folding operations. A bone folder, available in some craft and stationery stores, is in many ways preferable. (A bone folder is illustrated in Figure 28, Chapter 10.)

Steel ruler. For cutting and measuring operations. It should be at least 12" long and of substantial weight.

Hand drill and bit. A manual or electric drill are equally as usable. The bit should be 1/16".

Brushes. Two brushes are needed for applying paste and glue: a large brush (e.g., sash painting brush), which should be bridled by wrapping wire around the bristles at midpoint (as in Figure 21, Chapter 7); and a small artist's brush, which is used for applying a fine line of adhesive.

Sewing needle. Should be sturdy, with a large eye, such as a tapestry needle.

OPTIONAL TOOLS

Tin shears. For cutting binder board, as a substitute for the more cumbersome steel rule and sharp knife.

Try-square. To check the squareness of cut binder board. Also called a carpenter's square. (Do not confuse with a t-square, which is a drafting instrument.)

C-clamps. Necessary for one of several methods of using the drilling jig. Two clamps of the 6" variety are ideal.

Dividers. The most convenient method of checking board spacing when making the case.

Clothespin. Used only during the repair of dog-eared case corners.

Tweezers. Used only during page repair. Fine-pointed tweezers are best.

BASIC MATERIALS

Supercloth. A stiffened, gauze-like fabric used for hinges. Crinoline or cotton organdy can be used as well.

Book cloth. A coated fabric used to cover the case. Various coated papers may be substituted.

Binder board. A strong and lightweight board used to make the covers of the bound book. As a substitute, thin pieces of cardboard can be laminated (with less satisfactory results).

Endpaper material. Any lightweight paper of sufficient size, strength and flexibility will suffice. Binding supply houses sell fancy papers intended for use as endpapers.

Headbanding. A thin strip of silk with alternating bands of contrasting colors. Headbanding may be omitted entirely.

Coated cardboard. Cardboard coated with paper on one or two sides (sometimes called poster board or railroad board) is necessary for constructing the slipcase.

Gummed paper. In strips, used in determining the position of binder boards in case. Envelope flaps or mailing labels can be used.

Wax paper. Convenient pre-cut sheets are available in some craft shops. Wax paper by the roll can be used for any application in this book.

Sandpaper. Coarse and fine grades.

Thread. Medium (button) grade.

Rubber bands. Various sizes, especially large.

Cellulose acetate tape. "Scotch" tape is used when making the slipcase.

Adhesives. Two different varieties of adhesives are essential to bookbinding. The first, which always will be referred to as *paste*, is relatively slow drying and thus errors can be corrected. You may use many different preparations, among them wallpaper paste (mixed from a powder), library paste and various flour and water concoctions. The second variety of adhesive will always be referred to as *glue*. Any kind of runny white glue (e.g., "Elmer's") will be suitable. Glue dries much faster than paste and errors are corrected only with difficulty. Mucilage should *not* be substituted for either of these adhesives—it is too brittle when dry.

Also necessary in profusion are rags, jars, scrap paper of various sizes and old newspapers.

OPTIONAL MATERIALS

Ribbon. Narrow silk ribbon for the bookmark.

Page repair tissue. Available from library supply houses. Various forms of "mending tissue" may be substituted. Lens cleaning tissue, available in any camera store, is a good substitute.

India ink, transfer letters, spray acrylic, gold foil and other materials are used for optional embellishment of the case (Chapter 6).

SPECIAL EQUIPMENT

Instructions are furnished below for the construction of three pieces of equipment. The drilling jig and finishing press are indispensable. The box mortise is merely a convenient stand over which to suspend the other two pieces of equipment. It is unnecessary if you have a hole in your workbench large enough to accommodate the press and jig, or if you can devise some other method of suspension (e.g., a vise or clamps).

The finishing press is composed of two pieces of wood which are held together with bolts, washers and wing nuts (Figures 3 and 4). The length of the bolts is optional, depending on the maximum thickness of the material you expect to bind. The boards should be 1" in thickness, 14" long and 5" wide. This length will accommodate material with a maximum dimension of 11". Drill more than one set of holes so that the bolts can be placed in various positions to assure maximum tension with books of varying height. The inside surface of the boards should be covered with lightweight cardboard (through which the holes are also drilled) to prevent unused holes from embossing the material being bound.

You will note that one edge of each board is beveled at 45° and that the corners are indented. The former feature is necessary for the rounding and backing operation, while the latter permits the press to rest on the box mortise. On the opposite edge of each board is mounted a metal strip

FIGURE 3

FIGURE 4

FIGURE 5

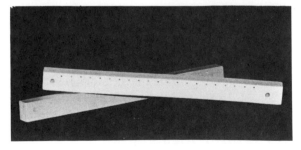

FIGURE 6

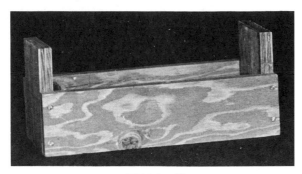

FIGURE 7

1/8" in thickness and approximately 1/2" in width (Figure 5). 1/8" of each strip is permitted to extend over the edge of the board. Thus the boards can be turned smooth-side-inward for standard pressing operations, or flange-side-inward during formation of the hinge.

The drilling jig (Figure 6) consists of two strips of wood, with holes drilled only in the front strip. The other strip is a backing strip into which the drill bit will barely bite after having penetrated the contents of the book. The backing piece should be replaced from time to time, as it becomes riddled with holes. The strips should be 12" long, 1" wide and 1/2" thick. The series of holes drilled in the front piece should be at intervals of 1/2". Be sure to drill the holes perpendicular to the face of the strip, not angled to one side or the other. A larger set of holes is drilled at both ends of *both*

strips to accommodate bolts, washers and wing nuts, as in the finishing press.

The box mortise (Figure 7) is constructed of odd pieces of scrap. It need not have a bottom if the corners are carefully braced, but it should be square and sturdy enough to sustain continued pounding from above.

The box mortise may be constructed of four pieces of 3/4" plywood of sizes that can usually be purchased as scrap-ends in a building supply store. The end pieces are 4½" wide and 6" high, cut perfectly square. The side (or long) pieces are 3½" high and 13½" long, also cut perfectly square. These dimensions can vary slightly but the opening, or mortise, must be of sufficient length to allow both the clamp and the drilling jig to rest on the top as shown in Figures 8 and 11. The box has no bottom and when made of plywood no thinner than 3/4" it will have ample rigidity.

In constructing the box the sides overlap the end pieces in simple butt joints. First place one side perfectly in line over the edges of the two end pieces (see Figure 7) and drive two or three common 2" nails through the ends of the side piece into the precise center of the edges of the two end pieces. Then turn the box over and attach the other side piece onto the two ends in the same manner. There is no actual need for screws to be used, which would require drilling and countersinking, because the mortise box is intended to be functional rather than decorative.

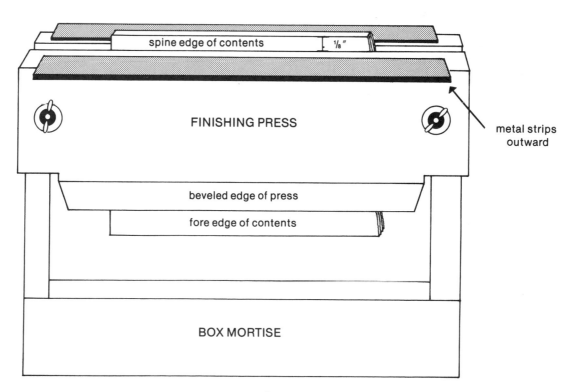

FIGURE 8

3
Preparing the Contents for Binding

We want to begin the binding process at a common starting point: with an alignable stack of loose pages or signatures, relatively free of glue or other encumbrances. Naturally, this requires a number of slightly different initial procedures, according to the type of book with which we begin. In this chapter we will outline the preparations needed for the bindings described in the previous chapter, plus a number of special cases that one is likely to encounter.

It is recommended that you read this chapter in its entirety when giving this book an initial reading, so that you will be familiar with all preparations. After that, you will want to refer only to the section that applies to your particular project. If you are binding a blank book, that is, a collection of loose, blank pages to be used as a journal, drawing book, etc., you will want to skip this chapter entirely.

Signature-bound paperbacks. Using a sharp knife, cut off the front and back covers at the hinge, as close to the spine as possible without damaging the first or last pages. Save the front cover, as you may want to use it later as a cover decoration on the bound book. To protect the contents during what is to follow, cut four sheets of typing (or scrap) paper to the size of the book pages. Place two of these sheets on either side of the contents. Fasten the book into the finishing press (square side up, metal strips outward) so that 1/8" of the spine protrudes (see Figure 8). Scrape away as much of the paper spine and adhesive as possible with the edge of a knife until the signatures become loose. Work with care, but don't be concerned if the signature folds are cut or if the stitching is broken. A mixture of one-half white glue and one-half water can be used to soften the old adhesive for removal. Dab it on with a brush and allow it to soak in for five minutes, then proceed with the removal. Another technique involves using coarse sandpaper, in addition to or as a replacement for the glue technique. The spine must be completely dry before rubbing it with the sandpaper.

When the spine is clean and the signatures loose, cut through the stitches and pull them out. Remove the book from the press, discard the protective sheets, and test whether the signatures will

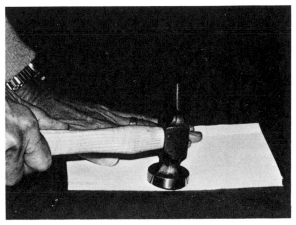

FIGURE 9

align squarely on the spine, top and bottom edges. A small amount of adhesive usually remains at a depth of 1/4" below the signature folds. This should be permitted to remain as it contributes to the square alignment of the book. If the folds of the signatures have become swollen with moisture, two things should be done. First, lightly pound these folds with a hammer as shown in Figure 9. Next, clamp the spine tightly in the finishing press until it dries, protecting both sides of the contents with a sheet of wax paper.

Hold the book down tightly on the bench top with 1/8" of the spine protruding over the edge (or use a block of wood with a straight edge). With a hammer, pound the spine lightly from head to tail. Turn the book over and repeat the procedure. This is intended to break the paper grain and cause light creases in the outside signatures, which will make for easier backing later in the bookbinding process.

Perfect-bound paperbacks. Remove covers and clamp in press as described above. Remove adhesive with knife, glue mixture and/or sandpaper. If the pages do not readily come apart into single sheets through application of these procedures, or if the paperback has developed a concave spine, remove the book from the press and cut the contents through the spine into artificial signatures of six to eight pages each. Begin cutting at the center of the spine and work your way outward, being careful not to damage individual pages. Make sure that these signatures will align perfectly along spine, top and bottom edges before proceeding. Hold the book tightly on the bench top with 1/8" of the spine protruding over the edge and pound lightly from top to bottom. Flip the book over and repeat the procedure.

Clothbound books. Make sure you are familiar with the repairs outlined in Chapter 10 of this book, and that you really want to recase your book rather than making repairs that can be accomplished with the case in place. If you decide to remove the case, you may want to salvage the front and back covers of the book with endpapers intact. Even if the covers are unsightly, they can often be recovered and reused. This saves time and money by eliminating the need to cut new binderboard. Sometimes the endpapers also may be reused.

Open the front cover and turn back the free endpaper. While pressing on the body of the book, pull the free portion of the endpaper slowly and firmly until it pulls away from the contents of the book and the supercloth hinge is exposed. If the free portion of the endpaper has been attached to the contents with an excessive amount of glue, you may have to slice carefully between the pages to expose the hinge. Next, cut the exposed hinge with a sharp knife (Figure 10). Repeat this procedure with the back cover. The case should now come free of the contents. Scrape off the spine strip on the exposed spine, and proceed according to the instructions in the signature-bound paperback section, above.

Saddle-stitched books. Remove the staples, using a staple remover, blunt knife or screwdriver. This can be a dangerous procedure, so be careful. Separate the pairs of pages, and refold them, if necessary, so that both halves of each pair align

exactly. Reinforce the fold with a bone folder or blunt knife. Slit each pair at the crease with a sharp knife. The result should be a set of single pages, all of the same dimensions, ready to be bound. Make certain that the pages are in the right order before proceeding.

Following are two special cases, frequently encountered, that require slightly different preparations:

National Geographic Magazine. *National Geographic*, as well as several other thick periodicals, is wire-stitched down through the pages at about 1/8" from the spine. Prepare such material for cloth binding by first removing the staples. Slice off the covers at the hinge. When binding a number of magazines together in a single volume, you will probably want to treat the covers as pages. Place each magazine separately in the press for preparation, with protective scrap on either side. Scrape the hinge with a sharp knife. Remove the magazine from the press and cut into artificial signatures as described in the section on perfect-bound paperbacks, above.

Very thin pamphlets. When dealing with saddle-stitched material of only a few paired pages, *do not* cut apart the halves of each pair. Prepare a strip of lightweight book cloth in the same manner as the supercloth hinge described in the next chapter. Fold it over the paired pages of the pamphlet and sew it with the pages. Do not attach headbanding. Also omit the step in which the spine is rounded and backed with the hammer (Chapter 4). From this point on, the book cloth hinge can be treated as though it were a supercloth hinge of the conventional variety. If the pages of your pamphlet chance not to be paired, create synthetic pairs by folding the spine edges together and gluing them.

FIGURE 10

4

Drilling, Sewing, Rounding & Backing

After carefully aligning the pages, fasten the contents into the drilling jig, holding the book tightly in place with wing nuts. The book should be positioned so that the holes will be drilled 1/4" from the spine edge, and so that the first and last holes will be about 1/2" from the head and tail of the spine. If you are using an electric drill, or if you are using a hand drill and can enlist the services of a helper (to hold the jig during drilling), suspend the jig over the box mortise (Figure 11). If you lack both an electric drill and a helper, devise

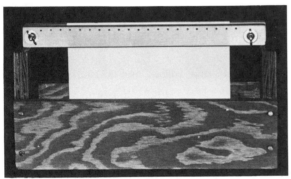

FIGURE 11

FIGURE 12

some method of clamping the jig to the bench top or holding it in place with a vise. Figure 12 illustrates such an arrangement.

Using a 1/16" drill bit, drill through the contents at intervals of 1" (every other hole in the jig). The depth of the drill bit should be adjusted in the chuck so that it barely bites the backing strip after having penetrated the pages of the book. After drilling, remove the book from the jig. You are now ready to begin sewing.

You will need an ordinary sewing needle and white or transparent thread of the medium or "button" grade. The sewing method is backstitching. Begin at the middle hole (see Figure 13), pushing the needle down through the book and leaving at least 3" of thread protruding from the top of the hole. Moving toward the head of the spine, bring the needle up through the next hole and go down through the one after that. Continue until you reach the last hole, and then reverse directions, sewing toward the tail of the spine. This time, skip the starting hole. Reverse directions again when you reach the hole nearest the tail of the spine. Finish by bringing the needle back through the starting hole. Keep the thread taut during this process, but do not pull it so tight that the pages buckle to the slightest extent. Tie the two threads and trim them so that the knot and thread ends are inside the middle hole.

Cut two pieces of wax paper to be 3" wider than the book, and place them on either side of the book so that the excess 3" extends beyond the spine edge. Fasten the book and wax paper into the beveled edges of the finishing press, with 3/16" of the spine protruding. The 3" of wax paper on each side should flop over the edges of the press. Make sure that the protruding edge of the spine is precisely parallel to the edges of the press. Place this assembly over the box mortise to begin the rounding and backing process.

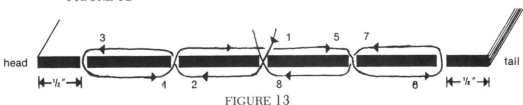

FIGURE 13

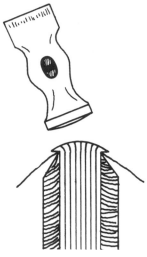

FIGURE 14

With a hammer, tap along the center of the spine, allowing the hammer to glide toward the front and back of the book as you strike with glancing blows (see Figure 14). Work from the head of the spine to the tail and then reverse the process. The outer portions of the spine will gradually bend over the edges of the press and the middle portions should mushroom without being biased in either direction. Proceed with care, so a perfect symmetry is achieved along the spine and from side to side. If the spine offers too much resistance, strike harder and dampen the spine slightly with water. When you are finished, the spine should be slightly rounded. Remove any additional layers of paper or adhesive that may work loose during this process. Leave the book in the press for the next step.

Cut a piece of supercloth 2" shorter than the length of the spine and 4" wider than the width of the spine. Carefully spread white glue the entire length of the spine, working it in well with a brush and making certain that none of it runs down the top or bottom edges of the contents. This is best accomplished by beginning at the middle of the spine and working the glue towards the edges. Rub the glue in with your fingertips, and then repeat the process with another light coating of glue. Wipe your fingers clean on a damp rag. Quickly place the supercloth on the spine so that it is centered about 1" from the head and tail of the spine, and with 2" extending on either side of the spine.

This is the point at which to attach a ribbon bookmark, if you wish to do so. If not, go on to the next paragraph. Cut a piece of narrow ribbon to

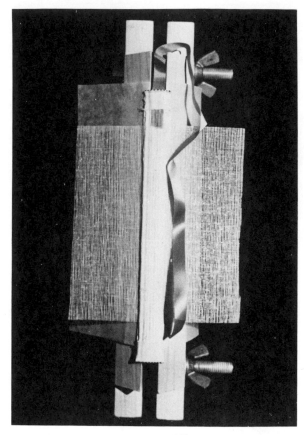

FIGURE 15

be 6" longer than the length of the book. The ribbon can be cut shorter after the book is completed, and for all further processes it will be folded into the center of the book. Glue the first inch of the ribbon to the head of the spine. The headbanding will be glued on top of it, as described in the next paragraph.

Cut two pieces of headbanding to be the width of the spine. Glue them to the head and tail ends of the spine so that only the colored portions extend over the top and bottom edges of the contents. Figure 15 shows the supercloth hinge and head and tail bands in place, with a bookmark attached.

Cut a piece of heavy paper the exact size of the spine and then snip a small piece off the end so that this strip fits exactly within the colored portions of the head and tailbanding. Apply a light coating of glue to one side of this strip while it rests on a piece of newspaper. Immediately discard the soiled newspaper and glue the spine strip over the supercloth on the spine. Set the book aside while still in the press to dry overnight.

5

Making the Case

Using a sharp knife and steel rule or a pair of tin shears, cut two identical pieces of binder board, with dimensions arrived at by the following formulas:

The width should be the width of the contents, measured from the fore edge of the contents to the edge of the spine, *plus* 1/8".

The length should be the length of the contents *plus* 1/4".

Make sure that the corners of these boards are perfectly square.

Using scissors, cut a piece of book cloth according to the following formulas:

The width should be double the width of the binder boards *plus* the width of the spine *plus* 2".

The height should be the height of the binder boards *plus* 2".

Cut a piece of heavy scrap paper to be the width of the spine and the same height as the binder boards.

Place the boards on the front and back of the contents so that they are exactly 1/16" from the spine edge and perfectly centered over the contents relative to the top and bottom edges. Place two rubber bands over this assembly lengthwise, being certain that the location of the boards remains the same. Cut two pieces of gummed paper 1/2" wide and 4" long. Dampen about 1/2" of one end of the first of these and affix it to the front cover about 1" from the spine and about 1/4 of the distance from the top of the book. Run the strip around the spine, keeping it taut. As you do so, press this strip (with a plastic ruler or bone folder) into the hinge on either side of the spine. Affix the other end of the strip to the back cover at exactly the same height as on the front cover. Repeat this procedure with the second strip, at a similar distance from the bottom of the book. Be very certain that the boards do not move during this procedure. After the strips have dried in place, remove the rubber bands. Set the contents aside until the next chapter.

Center the binder boards and strips over the inside of the piece of book cloth. The strips should be between the surface of the cloth and the binder boards. A roughly equal amount of fabric should protrude on all sides. Check to make sure that the boards are equidistant from each other at all points (this is most conveniently done with a set of dividers, as in Figure 16). Mark the location of all four corners of both boards on the book cloth with dark pencil marks. Mark a large L on the top of the lefthand board and an R on the top of the righthand board. These marks will help to relocate the boards on the cloth in precisely the same position and orientation for pasting. Remove the boards, tear off and discard the paper strips.

Have ready two stacks of newspaper, a damp rag, paste pot and brush. Place the book cloth, marked side up, on one stack of newspaper. Place one board, marked side down, on the other stack. Apply a thin layer of paste to the board, working the paste from the center to the edges. Place the board, marked side up and in the proper position, on the book cloth. Press it down firmly, and rub it with your hand. Repeat this procedure with the second board, after discarding the top sheet of newspaper. Lift up the cloth by the two top corners and turn it upside down. Check for air bubbles. If you find some, rub them to the edges of the boards with your fingers. Be careful not to stretch the cloth in doing so. Turn the cloth over (discarding a sheet of newspaper in the process) and check to make sure the boards are properly located. Apply paste to the spine strip and paste it in place between the boards, precisely equidistant from both.

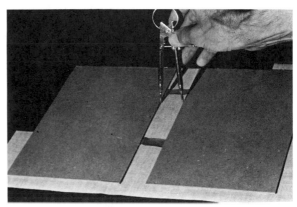

FIGURE 16

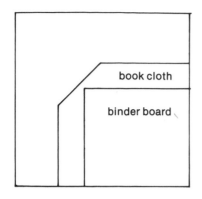
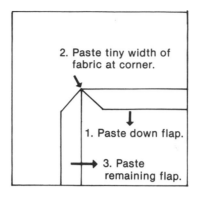
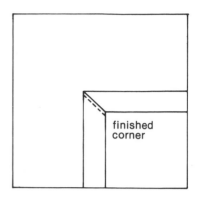

2. Paste tiny width of fabric at corner.

1. Paste down flap.

3. Paste remaining flap.

finished corner

book cloth

binder board

FIGURE 17

When preparing a case for very thin material, the following instructions apply: The boards are cut 1/2" wider than the contents and 1/2" greater in height. The step involving the fitting of the cloth to the spine and covers through use of rubber bands and paper strips is omitted. Rather, place the boards on a piece of book cloth (cut according to the formula at the start of this chapter), perfectly aligned and with 1/4" of space between them. Mark the position and orientation of the binder boards, as before. Paste the boards to the book cloth. Note that no spine strip is used between the boards. Continue as for a wider volume.

You are now ready to finish the case by folding the excess cloth around the boards, entailing formation of cloth corners at the outside corners of the boards. Many techniques can be used to form corners, two of which will be described here. It is recommended that you practice forming corners with some scrap material and board before you try it on the case.

The *mitered corner* (Figure 17) is neat, simple to make and sufficiently durable to withstand normal wear. Using scissors, angle-cut a piece of cloth from each of the four outside corners, so that the cloth remaining between the corner of the board and the angle-cut line is slightly greater in width than the thickness of the board. Apply a thin coating of paste to the top edge of the boards and the exposed surface of cloth constituting the top flap. Pull this flap over the edge and paste to the top surface of the boards. Rub the bubbles to

the edges, as before. Repeat with the bottom flap. Once again, remember to discard a sheet of newspaper after every pasting operation, to avoid staining the exterior of your case with adhesive.

Apply paste to the tiny width of fabric at the top and bottom lefthand corners and press them into place with fingernail or bone folder. Apply paste to the lefthand flap and press it into place. Repeat this procedure with corners and flap on the righthand side. Wipe all excess paste from the places where cloth has been adhered. Set aside for drying.

The *library corner* (Figure 18) is favored by libraries because of its extra durability. This results from the relatively greater quantity of fabric accumulated around the corner. To make the corner, apply paste to the protruding corner of fabric and fold it over the corner of the board. When all four corners have been pasted, paste and adhere the flaps as in the previous method.

Many other methods of corner folding are possible. You may want to experiment with corners of your own invention.

The next chapter contains information on alternate styles of binding and instruction on how to embellish books with lettering, ornaments, etc. Since these are all advanced techniques, you may want to skip the next chapter when binding your first few books. If you decide to try any of them, they must be accomplished at this point in the bookbinding process, that is, before the case is attached to the contents.

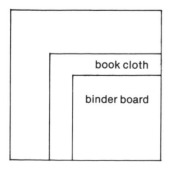
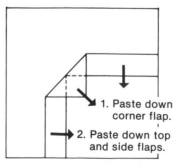

book cloth

binder board

1. Paste down corner flap.

2. Paste down top and side flaps.

finished corner

FIGURE 18

6

Embellishing the Book

The binding technique we have been describing is called *full cloth*. It is also possible to cover the case with a combination of materials such as cloth and paper, leather and cloth, or contrasting colors of cloth. With these methods, the more-durable material is used at the spine and/or the corners, the points at which the book receives the most wear. Using less-durable material on other exterior surfaces makes for greater economy and a pleasing variation in appearance. For a very rich-looking book, leather may be used at spine and corners, with a compatible color of cloth elsewhere.

A *half-cloth binding* has a cloth spine (Figure 19). The balance of the cover should be of a lightweight, flexible paper. Begin by covering the entire case with this paper, using the methods outlined in the previous chapter. Cut a strip of bookcloth to be considerably wider and slightly longer than the spine. Carefully paste this on the spine of the case, making certain that the same amount of material overlaps the front and back covers, and that the overlap line runs perfectly perpendicular to the top and bottom edges of the covers.

A *three-quarter cloth binding* has a cloth spine and cloth corners (Figure 20). Cut and paste a spine strip as in the above paragraph. Next, cut four triangular corners from the same material. Apply these corners by one of the methods used in the previous chapter for finishing corners. It is important to make sure that the four corners are all identical in appearance.

It is at this point that cover ornaments of any kind should be added to the case. These can con-

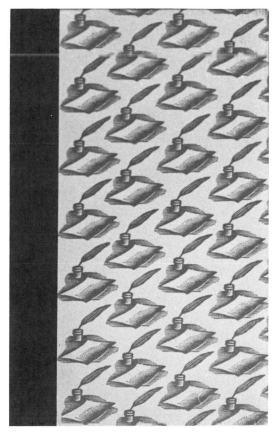

FIGURE 19

FIGURE 20

sist of labels bearing the author's last name and the title of the book, applied to the spine and/or the front cover. You can letter the labels by hand (india ink is recommended), with a typewriter or using pressure-transfer letters available in art supply stores. These labels should be carefully affixed using white glue, and any excess glue must be wiped off immediately with a damp rag. Labels which might smear can be fixed with spray acrylic before adhering. Spine labels should run down the spine, and begin about 1/2'' from the top of the spine. If you use a front cover label on a full cloth binding, you might want to create a depression in the front cover to keep the label from being damaged by rubbing. To do this, press a heavy card with the front cover in a vise immediately after finishing the case (while the paste is yet wet).

The depression should be slightly larger than the label you want to attach.

A variety of pre-gummed foil ornaments are available in many craft shops. These are normally used at the head of the spine. An electric pencil can be used with sheets of gold or silver foil to letter directly on the case of the book. Needless to say, this latter method requires much practice before it can be done with pleasing results.

As mentioned earlier, you can also decorate the front cover with the original cover of a paperback. It should be trimmed so that it can be centered on the front cover of the bound book, the same distance from every edge. Attach it with a conservative amount of white glue, once again being careful to immediately wipe off the excess with a damp rag.

7

Casing the Book

It is at this point that we attach the contents to the finished case. Have ready a stack of newspaper, wax paper, white glue, brush, damp and dry rags. Center the spine edge of the contents over the spine strip of the case, making certain that, if the case has been embellished, the head of the contents corresponds to the top of the case. Draw pencil lines onto the spine strip to mark the top and bottom edges of the contents. Carefully tip over the contents onto the right-hand side of the case, making sure that the contents moves neither up nor down in doing so (check by referring to the lines drawn on the spine strip).

Place a piece of newspaper between the exposed supercloth hinge and the contents. Apply white glue sparingly to the hinge, working from the spine edge to the newspaper (Figure 21). Slip two pieces of wax paper between the sheet of newspaper and the contents, and then pull out the sheet of newspaper and discard it. Check to see that the supercloth lies flat, without wrinkles. Quickly bring up the left-hand side of the case and press it down onto the supercloth hinge. Make certain the

edges of the left-hand (front) cover are precisely parallel to the edges of the contents. It is important that the above operations be done correctly the first time, since the rapid setting of the white glue makes a second attempt difficult.

Turn the book over and repeat these operations with the right-hand (back) cover of the book. Make sure that the front and back covers coincide perfectly.

The next step is called *pressing in*, and its object is to create those grooves which are the exterior manifestation of the hinges. This step should be performed as soon after gluing as possible to take advantage of the wet elasticity of the supercloth. Handle the assembly of case and contents with great care, so no rearrangement of the components occurs. Place this assembly in the finishing press (square side up, metal strips inward) so that the metal strips bite the front and back cover in the narrow space between the spine strip and binder boards (see Figure 22). If your entire case is paper-covered, interpose pieces of lightweight scrap between the blades of the press and the

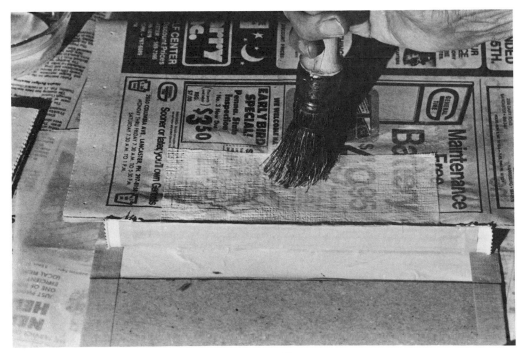

FIGURE 21

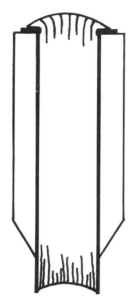

FIGURE 22

FIGURE 23

covers. Be certain that the edges of the press are precisely parallel to the spine. Suspend the press over the box mortise and dry overnight with the book in the press. After removing, the book should resemble the book in Figure 23. If the book is thick, the spine should be convex. In the next chapter we will describe how endpapers are inserted.

Special notes for binding very thin material: Since we did not round and back the spine edge in Chapter 4, the spine will be flat instead of rounded. Less pressure should be applied during pressing in, although faint grooves should still result at the hinges.

8

Inserting the Endpapers

Select a variety of paper suitable for use as endpaper, one that fulfills the following criteria: It must be flexible, durable and attractive. In addition, it must be of sufficient size. You will need two sheets that are the same height as a page of the contents, and at least twice its width. Heavy-grade wrapping paper, wallpaper and drawing paper are all usable. Handmade marbleized paper is available from some of the supply sources listed in the appendix, and is especially attractive. Also available (from Dover Publications) are a number of saddle-stitched books of dollhouse wallpaper and floor-coverings, and a book of marbleized paper for craft use.

Cut two sheets of this paper to be exactly the same height as the contents, and slightly more than twice the width of a contents page. Place the book on a stack of newspapers and open the front cover. Apply enough paste to half of the endpaper to adhere it to the inside of the front cover, so that the paper is 1/4" from the fore edge of the cover and aligned with the top and bottom of the adjoining page. If not perfectly positioned, the endpaper may be skidded into alignment, since the paste is relatively slow-drying. Use a damp rag to remove excess paste. Use your finger, and then a plastic ruler or bone folder, to crease the endpaper into the spine of the book. The half of the endpaper not adhered will protrude beyond the fore edge of the contents.

Place a sheet of wax paper between the halves of the endpaper. Using a fine brush, apply a small line of paste to the spine edge of the endpaper, where it faces the contents. This should adhere the endpaper to the contents, but not affect the free movement of the loose half of the endpaper. Remove excess paste with a damp rag. Repeat entire procedure with the back endpaper. Place the book on a flat surface with a heavy weight on top of it (a thick book is sufficient). Allow to dry for at least two hours.

Remove the wax paper, and check to see that the endpapers are properly joined to the covers and exterior pages of the contents. While the book is closed, draw a light pencil line along the first page of the contents onto the protruding front endpaper. Open the book and trim the endpaper along this line, using scissors (Figure 24). Repeat this procedure with the rear endpaper. Your book is now completely bound. The next chapter describes how to make a slipcase for the book.

FIGURE 24

9

Making a Slipcase

A *slipcase* is a box-like container for a book, designed to keep it clean and free from dust. Each slipcase must be custom-fitted to a book. It must be made of some sort of lightweight paper-covered cardboard. That variety known as *poster board* is covered on one side only. *Railroad board* is covered with paper on both sides. The paper covering, which will face inward, is necessary to prevent the cardboard from warping when finishing material is applied to the outside of the slipcase. The thickness of the paper-covered cardboard should be proportional to the size and weight of the book.

The slipcase will be made from two pieces of cardboard cut like those in Figure 25. They should be cut according to the formulas that follow. It will not be necessary to make any marks on the cardboard except for the fold marks.

On the half marked *Right*, sections A and C should be the same length as the width of the book, measured from the fore edge of the front cover to the outside edge of the spine. The width of A and C should be the same as the thickness of the book, including the covers. The length of B and D

should be the same as the height of the book. The width of B should be the thickness of the book.

On the half marked *Left*, the dimensions are computed in the same manner, except that an extra 1/16" is added to the widths of A, B and C. This extra width is added to compensate for the thickness of the cardboard when the left half is folded to enclose the right half.

Carefully draw pencil lines along the fold marks indicated in the diagram. Using a steel rule, run a bone folder or blunt knife along these lines. Make the folds, pressing each flap of cardboard against area D and reinforcing each fold with a knife or folder.

What will be the outside corners of the slipcase have been marked X on the diagram. It is necessary to snip off a slight amount of material at these corners, to avoid bunching when the corners are actually made. To do this, fold a pair of adjacent flaps against area D and cut off a slight amount of cardboard on the diagonal. Repeat this procedure with the other three corners.

You are now ready to begin assembly. Reverse the positions of the two halves, so that the B flaps

Paper-covered side

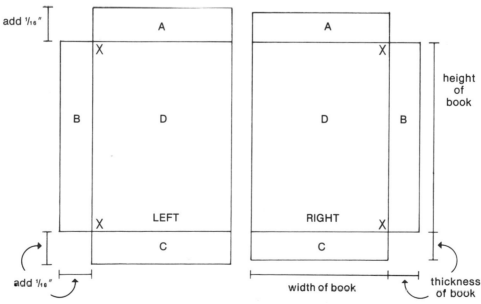

FIGURE 25

are next to one another. Using white glue adhere the larger *B* (now on the right) on top of the smaller *B* (now on the left). Place a wax-paper-covered weight on top of the flaps while they dry. Drying will be rapid.

Wrap the book for which you are making the case in two thicknesses of wax paper, making sure that the wrapping is tight around the book. Use "Scotch" (cellulose acetate) tape or masking tape to fasten the wax paper. Place the book fore edge downward on top of the joined *B* flaps, and bring the two halves of the case up around the book. Apply glue sparingly to the smaller *A* flap and press it over the larger *A* flap. Upend the entire assembly, so that the newly-glued joint is under the book. Put two heavy volumes on either side of the assembly so that it may dry in the upright position (Figure 26). Repeat this procedure with the flaps that remain.

You are now ready to cover the case with cloth and/or paper. The material, or combination of materials, can be selected to match or contrast with the material that covers the bound book. Unless indicated otherwise, leave the book (still covered with wax paper) inside the slipcase during these operations. We will first cover the top, spine and bottom of the slipcase with one continuous strip of cloth. Cut the cloth to be 2" longer than

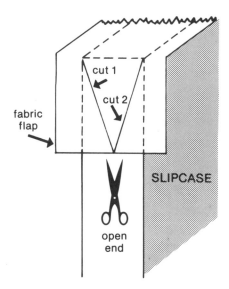

FIGURE 27

FIGURE 26

the length of these sides. The width should be 1" wider than the width of these sides. Apply a mixture of half glue, half paste to the top of the case, and adhere the strip so that 1" extends over the fore edge of the slipcase, and 1/2" extends on either side. Turn the case upside down; apply adhesive and adhere the strip to the remaining two sides. Once again, 1" of fabric should protrude over the fore edge. Remove the book and set it aside, but do not remove the wax paper.

The next operation is performed on the two ends of cloth protruding over the open end of the slipcase. On one of these make two cuts, each beginning at the center of the outer edge of the strip and ending at a corner of the case (Figure 27). Glue these flaps to the inside of the case, overlapping them. Pull the side flaps as tight as possible when gluing. Repeat for the flap on the other end of the case.

At each of the four corners bordering on the spine of the slipcase, snip out a small triangular piece of fabric. The triangles should extend up to, but not quite touch, the corners of the slipcase. Glue down all six flaps of cloth, overlapping the material at the corners. Reinsert the book, place the entire assembly on its side and weigh it down with a wax-paper-covered weight. Drying time should be minimal.

Next, cut another piece of cloth (or paper) which will be used to cover the sides of the slipcase and recover the spine. It should be 1/2" less than the height of the case and about 2" longer than the distance around the case, measured from open edge to open edge. With the book in place, apply glue to the fabric and wrap it around the two sides and spine of the slipcase so that a 1" flap protrudes over each of the fore edges. Keep the fabric taut during this process and immediately wipe off any excess glue with a damp rag. Remove the book and glue the two remaining flaps to the inside of the case. Replace the book and allow the entire assembly to dry overnight.

10
Repairs

Most repairs can be made with the case intact. These include replacement of endpapers and repair of torn pages and dog-eared corners on the case. Some repairs, such as replacement of the spine, require removal of the case. If a combination of repairs is required, and at least one entails removal of the case, all repairs will be easier to make with the case removed. When making repairs it is best to reuse undamaged parts of the book. If only the spine needs repair, the covers and endpapers may be reused. Repair of books is an excellent way to practice some of the circumscribed skills we have learned in this book.

Page repair. Page repair can be accomplished with the case intact, but it is somewhat easier to do with the case removed. Several different varieties of page repair will be described. Many make use of a special repair tissue available from library or binder's supply houses. This tissue is extremely thin and transparent, and not to be confused with the bulkier "mending tissue." (The latter may also be used, with less pleasing results.) Lens cleaning tissue is a good substitute. Never repair torn pages with Scotch tape, since the mastic will eventually ooze out and spoil the repair job.

To repair a torn page, where all parts of the page are intact, cut a piece of tissue 1/8" larger than the tear on all sides. Place a sheet of wax paper under the tear and carefully match up the two halves of the tear. Using your finger, spread a thin layer of paste over the tear. Drop the tissue onto the tear and smooth down with a bone folder (Figure 28). Place another sheet of wax paper over page and tissue. Close the book and allow to dry overnight. Remove the wax paper and trim protruding tissue with scissors. Using a tweezers, carefully tweeze off unattached tissue from around the tear.

If a piece of a page is missing, and the missing piece did not have print on it, find a piece of replacement scrap as much like the original in weight, color and texture as possible. Cut it to fit the gap and carefully bevel the edges of torn page and replacement with very fine sandpaper. It is easier to perform the beveling operation if you put an index card underneath. The beveled edges should fit together exactly. Apply paste and tissue as in the above paragraph. If the piece missing contained type, you may want to xerox the damaged page from a copy in the library and either replace the entire page (according to instructions in the next paragraph) or simply replace the fragment that is missing.

Pages that fall out of a book may be replaced by the following procedure. Put rubber bands around

FIGURE 28

those portions of the book preceding and following the page. Using a thin artist's brush, run a hairline of paste along both sides of the spine edge of the loose page. Insert the page and immediately remove the rubber bands. Allow to dry overnight. If the page has been torn out leaving a jagged edge, reconstruct the remainder of the loose page with scrap paper and then paste it into place as above. Make sure the reconstructed page is identical in size to the rest of the pages.

Endpapers. If an endpaper is slit at the fold, it may be repaired by adhering at the fold a narrow strip that matches or contrasts with the endpaper. If the endpaper is more badly damaged, remove it entirely. This may entail dampening, scraping and sanding operations on the half of the paper inside the cover. To make for a symmetrical book, both endpapers should always be replaced at once. Proceed to insert new endpapers as indicated in Chapter 8.

Corner repair. Dog-eared corners result from dropping a book on one or more of its corners. These may be repaired by carefully peeling back the endpaper and the book cloth from the damaged corner. A sharp knife will be helpful in this operation (Figure 29). Hold the book cloth out of the way with a clothespin. Place several thicknesses of wax paper under the corner and gently pound it with a hammer. Make a series of short slashes with a knife, perpendicular to the break and halfway through the binder board. Saturate

the surface with white glue and allow it to soak in. Wipe off any excess glue and cover the corner with several more thicknesses of wax paper. Pound it unrelentingly with a hammer. Replace wax paper top and bottom with fresh and allow to dry overnight with a heavy weight on top. Replace book cloth and endpaper.

If a corner is worn but not dog-eared, you might want to attach four new corners in the manner of the three-quarter binding (Chapter 6). The new corner material can be chosen to match or contrast with the cover material. In order to avoid tampering with the endpapers, the corners can be cut so as to fit up to, but not overlap, the attached half of the endpapers. Protect the endpapers with wax paper during gluing.

Spine replacement. If you want to replace the spine on a book, the case must be removed. This can be done without detectably damaging the endpapers. Cut through the hinges between the loose endpapers and contents; remove the case. Attach a new spine as if preparing a half-binding (Chapter 6). Scrape the spine of the contents, removing the old hinge. Attach a new hinge. If the endpapers are to be preserved, the ends of the hinge to be glued to the front and back covers can be shortened. The endpapers can then be pried up slightly to accommodate the new hinges. Reattach the repaired case to the contents as described in Chapter 7. Reglue the endpapers over the new hinge.

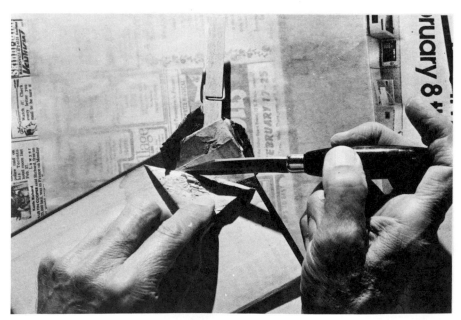

FIGURE 29

General Hints, Further Projects & Bibliography

Following are some general hints which will contribute to the success, both aesthetic and economic, of your bookbinding operation:

1. We have seen that the craft of bookbinding is dependent upon all sorts of scrap material. Begin to collect paper suitable for endpapers, cover material and replacement spines and corners. Keep a special lookout for discarded books—these can furnish a supply of blank pages of various sizes and weights, and it may be that other materials such as binder board and endpapers can be salvaged. Fragments of book cloth should always be saved for repair work.

2. Always work on a stack of newspaper of sufficient size. Conventional dailies should be cut into quarter sheets of tabloid size. Tabloids should be slit through the center fold. Perform each gluing operation on a fresh sheet, which should be immediately folded in upon itself and discarded.

3. Keep a jar of water and some rags handy whenever adhesives are used. Clean your brush immediately after each use. Glue spots (on book cloth, for example) are easy to clean with a damp rag if attended to without hesitation; once dry, they become a permanent blemish.

After you have acquired the requisite skills to produce a standard cloth binding, you may want to attempt more complicated projects. A series of books may be bound into matching bindings and slipcases. Or try a three-quarter binding using thin leather (called *skiver*) at corners and spine.

The above skills are within the purview of this book. There are additional skills, not taught here, that you may wish to acquire. These include trimming of pages, hand stitching of headbands, and gold leaf and tooled decoration of covers. To learn these and other skills, the books listed below will be helpful. All are available in paperback editions.

Cockerell, Douglas. *Bookbinding and the Care of Books.* New York: Taplinger Publishing Co., 1978.

Gross, Henry. *Simplified Bookbinding.* New York: Charles Scribner's Sons, 1976.

Lewis, A. W. *Basic Bookbinding.* New York: Dover Publications, 1957.

Sources of Supply

Following are reliable sources of supply for the home hobbyist. All these firms will furnish small quantities by mail order. A brief description of items available follows each entry.

Art Handicrafts Co., 3512 Flatlands Avenue, Brooklyn, New York 11234. Primarily a leather products company, they furnish fine-gauge leather suitable for cases, and genuine bone folders at a reasonable price.

Basic Crafts Co., 1201 Broadway, New York, New York 10001. Carries all basic equipment and supplies including printed and handmade marbleized endpapers.

Bookmaking Needs, 665 Third Street, Suite 335, San Francisco, California 94107. (415) 546-4168/1916 FAX. Carries bookbinding tools, supplies and how-to books. Free catalogue.

Brodart, Inc., 1609 Memorial Drive, Williamsport, Pennsylvania 17701. A supplier of library furniture and book repair and rebinding supplies. Also carries embellishing supplies of various sorts, including transfer foils and electric pencils.

Gaylord Bros., Inc., P. O. Box 4901, Syracuse, New York 13221. Primarily manufactures supplies for library book repair, including endpapers and wax paper in conveniently sized sheets, book cloth and brushes. They also manufacture a low-priced book press. Free catalogue.

Talas Division, Technical Library Service, 130 Fifth Avenue, New York, New York 10011. Carries a complete stock of traditional binding equipment and supplies, much of it custom-made and proportionately higher priced. One of the few companies which stocks a complete line for use of restorers. Free catalogue.